D1127557

Unthrifty Loveliness

Unthrifty Loveliness

Poems by Christopher Bursk

Word Poetry

© 2014 by Christopher Bursk

Published by Word Poetry
P.O. Box 541106
Cincinnati, OH 45254-1106

ISBN: 9781625491176
LCCN: 2014959048

Poetry Editor: Kevin Walzer
Business Editor: Lori Jareo

Visit us on the web at www.wordpoetrybooks.com

Acknowledgments:

These poems would not have made it to the light of day without the encouragement of Sandra Becker, Herb and Pamela Perkins-Frederick, and George Drew – and the inspiring example of their own intrepid poetry.

Thanks also to Steven Riel, Steven Huff, Betsy Sholl, April Ossmann, Jack Bursk, and Claire Rossini for asking hard questions about the poems, and to Philip Fried and *The Manhattan Review*, Israel Halpern and *Freshet,* Stacy Bodziak and *The Bellevue Literary Review* for publishing several of them. Thanks to Helen Wilson for her faith in my work. Thanks to Rona Cohen, Anne Tax, Peter Bridge, Robert Fishman, Sarah Halloran, and Elizabeth Young, for their faith in the power of words to heal.

Thanks to Janine Cole, Rosemary O'Keefe, Marylou Streznewski, Joanne Leva, Monica Flint, Christine McKee, Lorraine Lins, Camille Norvaisas, Katherine Falk, Deda Kavanagh, Marilee Morris, Laura Holloway, Cleveland Wall, Phyllis Purscell, Eric Hueber, Lavinia Kumar, Liz Rivers, Bill Wunder, Elizabeth Austin, Bernadette McBride, Bernadette Karpa, David Clark, and so many other brave poets who remind me, every time they write, what courage is.

Thanks to artist Danielle Bursk for the cover painting, *Cardiac Fire*.

For LB and MAB

Thou art all my art.

Table of Contents

1

What if you're eight and afraid
of almost everything – bread, your father,
recess, gym, music class, bridges, water
over your head, the smell of rain
before a storm, your grandfather's glass eye,
where to sit on the bus,
your uncle's inquisitive fingers,
the clicking shut
of a door, your mother's hands
on your throat, every reflecting
surface? Pay no attention to the face
in the mirror, but stare
at the wall behind you,
the painting of a boy asleep in a haystack.
Gaze long enough
and he will take your hand.

How You Learned to Read

Because you could hear your mother in the dusk
sobbing as if she'd just pulled a knife out of her,
you open *The Book of Knowledge,*
Volume 3, and start with H*ow to Draw a Jam Jar*
and do not stop till
What to Do with a Girl's Work Basket.
At your age, you don't need much light
to read. Or have to understand all the nouns
and verbs to know what they are saying.
The War Begun in a Rose Garden.
Little Picture Stories in French,
The Troubled Land Where a Child Was King,
Pictures of Leaves and Twigs
(Use Prussian blue, gamboge, a little light red.
Put Vandyke brown with the blue
and let the paper be damp – not too wet).
Something terrible will happen
if you don't pay attention to every word
in your grandfather's 1929 edition
of the *Book of Knowledge*, Volumes 1-20.
You know this the way you know nothing else
in your life. To keep yourself awake
you dig your nails into your arm as deep
as they go. T*he Struggle for a Continent,*
What Makes a Bee Hum?
Don Quixote and the Clouds of Dust,
The Procession of Treble Road,
Microbes That Do More Mischief than Wolves,

Two Fighting Clothespins,
Why Spiders Aren't Caught in Their Own Webs,
How Worms Breathe Underground,
What Keeps a Balloon Up,
Still More Little French Lessons in Pictures.
While your father downstairs is figuring out
how to keep your mother from killing herself
or you, you draw Sir Isaac Newton so close
to your face he could be whispering
to you or you to him.
That's the kind of reading you've always loved.

Visiting Hours

If you sit up as straight as you can,
maybe your mother will be proud of you
enough to introduce you to her friends –
the woman who smokes invisible cigarettes,
a two-legged man who stands like a bird on one.
If you whisper to her about the boy
you made up, your escapades with him,
she might stop worrying the cuffs
of her shirt, her fingers
rubbing out an imaginary spot on her sleeve,
tugging at a thread that's not there.
Maybe you'll tell her something
so important she'll have a reason to get better.
How yesterday you slayed a dragon.
How the day before you stopped the world
from spinning off its axis and into the sun.
You'll describe the flowers that grow
in the fields you and Alwyn explore;
how the pansies all have faces
just as she likes, how you and Alwyn
put down your bows and arrows
and undo your belts
till you're as naked as the wild animals
who wait for you.
Your secrets will be safe with your mother.
With whom would she share them?
The old woman who bites her lip till it bleeds,
the old man who rubs dirt into his face?
The doctors? It's your fault
your mother is here. You know it.
She knows it. On the hospital grounds

the birds dart from tree to tree, bragging
of their own adventures. Soon
your mother's fidgeting
with her collar as if it's too tight,
as if all her clothes hurt her.
You make a small hollow in the dirt
with the heel of your shoe.
There'll be no traveling today to other worlds.

A Fourth Grader's Concept of Justice

Some days you call him Rafe;
other days Ignacio; on rainy afternoons Ainslie;
in the dusk Poussaint. You tremble
in his presence like a candle flame
when a window's been opened in a room.
You're never ready for the back of his hand,
each slap questioning your face,
his fists' repeated reminders to your belly
that has no business going soft,
first one kick in your groin, then another,
as if that part of your body can never be damaged
enough. You don't want to be this boy
moaning on the floor, at the mercy of a man
determined to take from you
what he can, and you want to be this boy
more than anything else in the world.

Mirrors Useful for More Than You Might Think

1 – the pocket mirror

When your teacher looks at you –
as she often does – as if you're a stone
someone had dug up and asked her to teach
long division, it helps to know
you have another world
in your pocket. At least the door
into it. At recess you tilt your small mirror
till it fills with a tree you carry back to class.
Even though you know better
you like to believe that what a mirror looks at last
it keeps, so one day you have flowers
blooming in your pocket
and the next an insect buzzing there
whose twin still interrogates the dogwood outside.
You like that there are two of everything:
the rain drops gilding a leaf,
the leaf even more bejeweled in the glass.
The playground's smaller and less menacing
once it's enclosed in the rectangle
you've stuffed into your corduroys
so you can bear Clarkie Truesdale home with you,
Bobby Duggan next to your crotch
where he can't hurt you.
All that's required of you
is that you make sure the mirror doesn't drop
out of your hands as so much does
and splinter into more pieces than you could put
back together. You learn to walk

a certain way when carrying anything fragile,
but that's part of its beauty:
it could shatter all at once.

2 – full-length mirror

What do you need with a full-length mirror?
your mother wants to know.
What's so interesting about your body
you have to see it all at once?
You don't tell your mother
that you plan on stripping off pants and shirt
and waiting till the mirror decides
to be a door. You know one thing for sure:
you must be completely undressed
to walk through a mirror. You know also
there's a boy on the other side
so striking he doesn't need to wear clothes.
You go back and forth
between his world and yours.
Time passes so quickly on the other side
of the mirror that when you return
you're surprised to find it's only a half hour later.
And then one afternoon you wake
to your mother staring at you
sprawled on the floor before the mirror
and so still it must've been difficult for her
to tell if you were breathing or not.
She says nothing. Just closes the door
so softly you're not positive
she'd even been in your room.

When you come home from school
the next day, the mirror's gone.
You find it in the trash
smashed to so many pieces
she must've struck it with a hammer
over and over, so there'd be no way
you could put it back together.
You tried. How you tried!

2

Fair, kind, and true, is all my argument,
Fair, kind, and true, varying to other words;
And in this change is my invention spent –
Three themes in one, which wondrous scope affords.
Fair, kind, and true, hath often lived alone,
Which three, till now never kept seat in one
Sonnet 105

From: virginpoet <virginpoet@gmail.com>
To: lincolnbraxton <braxtonl@gmail.com>
Subject: Sonnet assignment
Date: Mon, Sept 15, 2003 7:46 pm
Attachment: Look what unthrift in the world doth spend

Dear LB,
Who'd suspect anyone so dead could be so horny? And over a boy he drools, simile by simile, and then enjoins not to fan his own flames with *self-substantial* fuel? Is this English class or Sex Ed.? Willie's reaching out from the grave to lay his grubby fingers on our family jewels and tweak them. And our teacher expects us to write a sonnet a day? I like what you said in class. "Perhaps you don't need to be gay to write sonnets but it must help to be a control freak." Right on, brother! Down with pentameter! Open the attachment.

Comrade in Arms

Is this why Shakespeare urges the Earl to get laid?
It's a question of managing resources, quality
control.
Iambic pentameter? No, regulated free trade.
Want to get a little wild? Do it frugally.
With a spondee. *Ten times thyself were happier*
If ten of thine ten times refigured thee.
As much as the Bard pretends to abhor waste,
apparently one Earl won't suffice. He multiplies
his teen
exponentially. Will's a veritable Xerox machine,
spitting out so many facsimiles he doesn't need
an actual boy; he'll have him always
within reach, kidnapped in each figure of speech.
Is that my hope too? To invest in so many
metaphors, my
most beloved fiction will finally come true?

From: virginpoet <virginpoet@gmail.com>
To: lincolnbraxton <braxtonl@gmail.com>
Subject: Sonnet assignment
Date: Tues, Sept 16, 2003 10:02 p.m.
Attachment: Do I envy these jacks that nimble leap

Dear LB,
Assigned the sonnets, did you expect a lecture on masturbation, a topic on which, it turns out, the Bard's quite versed? *No love toward others in thy bosom sits/ That on himself such murd'rous shame commits.* Even from the grave the Bard brings his beloved to his knees, cramming hyperbole down the boy's throat and filling his mouth with spondee. A posthumous blowjob. Should the kid refuse, he's a schmuck forever. But the Bard of Avon gets to screw long after he's died. *Look*, Will brags, *I can still get my pentameter up!* 'Tis true, each sonnet rises to the occasion, engorged with pride.

Your Classmate and Reluctant Sonneteer

Maybe the tongue doesn't need another body
to enjoy sex; it'll make do with the mind:
double entendres prove far more sanitary
than cunnilingus, no STDs from a sonnet. Yes,
someone's lips would be nice, but for a little
assonance upon which to chew the word *fellatio*
does suffice. *Since saucy jacks so happy are in this*
Give them thy fingers, me thy lips to kiss.
No better than the tongue at the bawdy pleasures
of a trope. In my iambs my jacks do *nimble leap,*
yet fumbling with my zipper and a girl's bra
in a car's backseat, I've no hope of any acrobatics.
All I do in the dark is apologize and grope,
apologize and grope. Then grope some more.

From: virginpoet <virginpoet@gmail.com>
To: lincolnbraxton <braxtonl@gmail.com>
Subject: Sonnet assignment
Date: Wed, Sept 17, 2006 9:38 pm
Attachnent And all in war with Time for love of you

Dear LB,
A sonnet a day? Who is Mr. V to require us to get naked? Similes have a knack of making one lie, then confess, get dolled up only to end up undressed. I'm learning the risks of rhyming: delaying and desiring. I never suspected two letter words wielded such seductive powers as if *as if* could lure a boy to pluck flowers normally he'd not be caught dead admiring. Attached is my latest attempt. I hate to confess this, but I actually liked writing it, though I'm not going to be bullied into that fascist a b a b, c d c d, e f e f g g.

A Now Not Completely Virgin Poet

Rome's burning, and to pass history I've an hour
to say why, but I'm having too much fun fiddling
with caesuras to worry over Christians.
If Nero had his priorities, I've mine. Right now
it's not taking exams but succumbing to an orgy
of iambs: *Lo in the orient where the gracious*
light
Lifts up its burning head. The sun riots
lasciviously in a girl's hair, its wanton excesses
travel down a boy's neck. Who cares if I flunk
Western Civ.? The greatest name in English
literature's
ignited by a kid my age, so why can't I blaze
a little too? Ah, combustible desire. Locked
in a sonnet I'll be as inflammatory as I wish.
At last I've a license to play with fire.

From:	virginpoet <virginpoet@gmail.com>
To:	lincolnbraxton <braxtonl@gmail.com>
Subject:	Sonnet assignment
Date:	Thurs, Sept 18, 2003 8:40 pm
Attachment:	When in disgrace with fortune and men's eyes

Dear Sir Walter Raleigh,
"Any more similes comparing a boy to a rose and we'll all turn queer," you shouted out today in class. Where does Mr. V get off saying that maybe we've more in common with the Bard than we'd like to admit: *Football and sonnets, dear class, recklessness with rules, the maximum utilization of a confined space.* You do have my e-mail address, right? I promise I won't let anyone see your replies. I just thought you might want to talk about this assignment with someone in case you're struggling with it like I am. Maybe send me one of your sonnets.

Sir Philip Sidney

Imagine Shakespeare putting on cleats?
Courting disgrace with every kick-off?
To prove oneself again and again and do it
by keeping one's eyes on someone else's thighs:
football all chaos, calamity, and carousing
in a contained space, dirt the perfect disguise.
Where else is a boy assigned to grab a boy
by the hip? Licentiousness unleashed in four
downs/fourteen lines, consonants eluding each
other's grip
one rhyme searching out the other; tackler
pursuing ball carrier like a long-lost brother;
collisions
more concussive because of what gets in the way;
signal calling perfecting the art of the pause:
each punt, each final couplet, our escape clause.

From: virginpoet <virginpoet@gmail.com>
To: lincolnbraxton <braxtonl@gmail.com>
Subject: Sonnet assignment
Date: Fri, Sept 19, 2003 7:56 pm
Attachment: With old woes new wail my dear time's waste

Dear LB.
Okay, I'm starting to worry about Mr. V. What kind of teacher breaks into tears just because of a poem? Please open the attachment. Are you getting these e-mails? I know, I know. Who's home on Friday nights?The answer is obviously me.

Are you there

One minute our teacher is helping Shakespeare
and the midday sun get us ready for a nap
and the next he's weeping over a caesura.
...*with old woes new wail my dear time's waste*.
his eyes brimming till sorrow's a secret
his body refuses to keep anymore. There are rules
for everything in school but not for when
your teacher sobs so hard he grabs hold
of the windowsill. It was like watching a tree
lose its composure. Or a wave rear, only to realize
it must irrevocably break on the shore.
Mr. V can't be that far in age from us. A decade?
What more can a man suffer in ten short years,
grief he's paying now *as if not paid before?*

From: virginpoet <virginpoet@gmail.com>
To: lincolnbraxton<braxtonl@gmail.com>
Subject: Sonnet assignment
Date: Sat, Sept 20, 2003 9:37 pm
Attachment: So shall I live supposing thou art true

Dear LB,
Since you haven't responded, I am not sure why I'm still e-mailing you. But then again, we've no record of the Earl's text messages back. Maybe the Bard never actually clicked the send button. You want to know who I am?

Here's a hint

Friday in the locker room, last refuge of mildew
and mold, hothouse of exotic blossoms opening,
Shakespeare made sense, finally: all those similes
next to me, in slow motion, unfolding
and blooming. No wonder I've trouble
lifting weights. I'm too busy searching for
metaphors
for your skin, that disarming white
of an amaryllis. As if a flower had decided
to flex its muscles, suit up, and start at
quarterback.
On the field, I pluck you. It's my job, a linebacker,
by definition a stalker. Is this why I joined the
team?
In my mind I'm not sacking you. We're having
a fling. It's better than any wet dream.
Maybe that's why I've never made first string.

From: virginpoet <virginpoet@gmail.com>
To: lincolnbraxton <braxtonl@gmail.com>
Subject: Sonnet assignment
Date: Sun, Sept 21, 2003 9:52 pm
Attachment: These hours that with gentle work did frame.

Dear LB,
The bad news is that you've haven't e-mailed me back. The good news is that you haven't e-mailed me back. You might demand I stop harassing you with sonnets. Is this how Emily Dickinson, one of Mr. V's favorites, felt? Yes, after Saturday's game, I went home and wrote a sonnet. This is getting out of hand, I know. Some people go to church, Sundays; I spend my Sabbath with tropes. Nope, I don't give up. What if I turned this poem into Mr. V.? What is he going to make of my extra credit assignment? That I've turned gay? Maybe he'll just think I'd fall for anyone to get an A.

I'm nobody. Who are you?

What is the use of worshiping your knees' hollows
or dedicating an entire French class to your ankles?
The chances of me ever laying my hands on you
are as likely as my getting a blow job from a tulip
or inviting a rose to my house to shoot hoops.
Maybe I've been reading too much Shakespeare.
Do I really expect to pull off a miracle in study hall
gaze till your too solid flesh distills into pure
thought, the way a rose's scent is stoppered
in a bottle? *A liquid prisoner pent in walls of glass.*
You, shrunk to fit a chalice, a sonnet to decant
on private occasions? The eyes have long practice
at transubstantiation, persuading blood into wine
and back: in *their* distillery nothing they can't
refine

From: virginpoet <virginpoet@gmail.com>
To: lincolnbraxton<braxtonl@gmail.com>
Subject: Sonnet assignment
Date: Tues, Sept 23, 2003 11:30 pm
Attachment: Ruin hath taught me thus to ruminate

Dear LB,
In my backpack I carry the history of the human race. From fire to hydrogen bomb, from Plato to plutonium.. I hope you are reading what I send you and hope you are not. There can be ruin in rumination.
Resigned

If I'm locked into iambs, I am free
of the Crimean War and profoundly dead
Socrates. *Focus*, our teachers say,
so I do: on the tilt of your head, the way light
manages even in a locker room to locate
the small of your back. Does it make me queer
to prefer it to all those diagrammed plays
on the board, a coach ranting like King Lear
Shakespeare chose to gild a boy's face.
In my sonnets I elaborate on a kid's ass,
the body's extra credit, both means and ends.
A sonnet's a hall pass. I'm at liberty to wander
from what tragedies loom ahead to what descends,
that bonus, ineffably sloping behind us.

From: virginpoet <virginpoet@gmail.com>
To: lincolnbraxton<braxtonl@gmail.com>
Subject: Sonnet assignment
Date: Tues, Sept 23, 2003 12:07 am
Attachment: Or shall I live your epitaph to make

Dear LB,
My #2's tired of sacrificing itself for love. *Stop while ahead*, it warns at the sentence's beginning as if it's seen what's coming: more inanities, more stumbling. Clichés? Not robbery perhaps, but certainly rental, and so the Ticonderoga's breaking in the middle of a metaphor seems hardly coincidental. Apparently graphite has little patience for the Byronic, especially right before midnight. It's had enough of poems by boys like me who find everything ironic as if fate exists for the sole purpose of trapping seventeen-year-olds. *Act your age*, the pencil scolds and proves its point, at 11:38 pm, by snapping.
The Ticonderoga Kid

Is this why the Bard butters up his boyfriend
as if he's toast, slathers the Earl's hips
with hyperbole, greases his groin till the lad, lubed
with similes, slips easily between millions
of lips? Easy to swallow a lover if he's nothing but
poetry, a little snack, a logarithm to graph.
If he's plain geometry then there's no messy
aftermath. Even the most ardent French kisser finds
spit hard to adore. There's no mucous
lining metaphor. Shakespeare doesn't offer his boy
eternal breath; he entombs him in a sonnet.
Iambic interment. Want love to endure? Embalm
your darling. Keep him/her pure.

From: virginpoet <virginpoet@gmail.com>
To: lincolnbraxton<braxtonl@gmail.com>
Subject: Sonnet assignment
Date: Wed, Sept 24,2003 9:16 pm
Attachment: So oft have I invoked thee for my muse

Dear LB,
Why after all these years of undressing not that many lockers away from you, should I suddenly start exposing myself to you – at least metaphorically? I hadn't expected to say all I have. Hell, before I said all this I didn't even know I thought it. This is our last year together in school, my last chance to watch light track you down to study hall. Maybe I just wanted you to know who I am without you knowing who I am.

Thine eyes have taught the dumb to sing.

Thou art my art. Perhaps Shakespeare wasn't gay,
just greedy, lovesick not only for the Earl, but for
all he inspired: the Bard's pen far more engorged
than his prick, a foreplay the mind engages in
long before the lower extremities do: a tinkering
with trochees, anapest's unexpected arousal.
So sonnets are useful for something.
Ah, desire! It's one thing to become infatuated
with flames, another to stick a hand in the fire.
Really I only longed to rest my head
in your lap. When we're apart, your soft skin's
so much softer. Close up, you're just you, but
miles away *you* transform into fragrant, silky,
irresistible *thou*. *Thou art all my art.*

From: virginpoet <virginpoet@gmail.com>
To: lincolnbraxton <braxtonl@gmail.com>
Subject: Sonnet assignment
Date: Thurs, Sept 25, 2003 9:23 pm
Attachment: Then should I spur, though mounted on the wind

Dear LB,
Who wants to appear as big a goofball as the poets in his lit. book? Shakespeare, for example, with his pants down, so famously horny he hops out of his saddle and hotfoots to his honey, outrunning his steed, a cowboy with an erection (talk about the cart before the horse!). Who expected such manure from such a master? But maybe one can't take flight without flapping one's wings and looking like a fool. What if the Bard hadn't been willing to risk everything for the sake of a rhyme? Maybe that's what he has to teach a young man like me: it's possible to be both ridiculous and sublime.

Certainly Ridiculous, Hardly Sublime Me

Inverse? Converse? Obverse?

No, perverse! Remember how we tormented
our sophomore math teacher whose hands shook
and whose tongue worried his lips until one day,
without warning he made a nude woman
appear in Geometry class. Out-Eucliding
Euclid, he expanded her coordinates
till her mammary glands and ass grew and grew
so gargantuan she threatened to topple
off the board and onto us. Then he pointed
to the formulae he'd surrounded her with,
their seemingly infinite complications, curves
elegantly bisected with x's and y's. *Now, students,*
tell me which one will endure. So there are more
ways to have sex than I suspected.

From: virginpoet <virginpoet@gmail.com>
To: lincolnbraxton <braxtonl@gmail.com>
Subject: Sonnet assignment
Date: Fri, Sept 26, 2003 9:42 pm
Attachment: A man in hue all hues in his controlling

Dear Locker 206,
If you haven't already guessed, I'm responsible for the picture slipped inside your locker last week. When you see that boy painted by Sir Joshua Reynolds, don't you feel you are gazing in a mirror? Apparently you existed centuries before you were born, and apparently I was born to do what a mirror does so much better.

Locker__________

Grow your hair to your shoulders,
trade in your football pads for plush
and let yourself tip slightly, with the help
of a good walking stick, your arm
outstretched so the light can admire the cut
of your velvet coat, and you could pass
for the boy on page 416 in *Eighteenth Century Art*.
Even Dr. Johnson might think you'd stepped
off his friend's palette and taken life.
It's never too late to learn, even for the author
of *The Dictionary*. I wish for you
what I wish for Reynolds' lad: a career
worthy of one the sun knows not to burn,
a family of consolations, wisdom for a wife.

From: virginpoet <virginpoet@gmail.com>
To: lincolnbraxton <braxtonl@gmail.com>
Subject: Sonnet assignment
Date: Sat, Sept 27, 2003 9:42 pm
Attachment: Farewell, thou art too dear for my possessing

Dear LB,
Why? Is that all you can type back after all this time. Not *Stop*. Not *Tell me more*. Not *I showed your e-mails to my sister and she says you're crazy*. Just *W-h-y?* Are three letters all you can manage?*Why?* Why did I choose you of all people? Why am I molesting you with all these sonnets? Why do all my similes, those sycophants, fawn over you? Why does the light travel the universe just to admire its lovely extrapolations in your hair? Why don't I at least address you by your full name?

You must suspect by now who I am

If you're only initials, you're just a kid
I scrimmage, but if I give in to each ***b*** and ***t***
and ***n*** and ***x*** of your full name,
I might get greedy for the whole alphabet
of your body, just as after a tackle, my fingers
hesitate to relinquish you. I'm even jealous
of the light when its finds your face and signs
its name with a flourish. It's no wonder I fell
for a boy who, even when he laughs, looks
about to cry, as if someone slapped you long ago
and you're waiting for that hand
again, its welt on your cheek, a beauty mark.
Maybe that's why you tilt your head
just so. So the light will let you go?

From: virginpoet <virginpoet@gmail.com>
To: lincolnbraxton<braxtonl@gmail.com>
Subject: Sonnet assignment
Date: Sun, Sept 28, 2003 9:42 pm
Attachment: Then thou, whose shadow shadows

Dear Doppelganger,
Sometimes I think maybe there are two of you. The one who sits a few desks away from me in ______ and in ________ and the one to whom I've sent all these sonnets. What hubris. At exactly 9:42 each night to sneak into your bedroom, e-mail by e-mail as if I were the moon and had the right to flatter you.

First person singular

Reading the sonnets, did I grow enamored
of you because it seemed a Shakespearean thing to
do? Ah, unrequited love. Night and day
it keeps my hands and heart and eyes busy.
How better to give my meaningless life meaning
than with a little anguish? Maybe
I'll get around to girls but for now
I choose a boy the same age as the Bard's
over whom to languish. Yes, you, *Lincoln*
Braxton. Even your name Elizabethan.
The proper language for love?
The Queen's English. Passion's too important
to be trusted to anything as common
and promiscuous as *you. Thou shalt be true.*

From: virginpoet<virginpoet@>gmail.com>
To: lincolnbraxton<braxtonl@gmail.com>
Subject: Sonnet assignment
Date: Mon, Sept 29, 2003 8:48 pm
Attachment My name be buried where my body is

Dear Lincoln Braxton:
Maybe it's a good sign you wish to know my name. Or are you planning to turn me in and let the proper authorities deal with my similes? *Thus have I had thee as a dream doth flatter/ In sleep a king, but waking no such matter.*

Forgive me if I stage your death every night;
each sonnet, an excuse to breathe life back into you,
my mouth so close to the page I'm almost giving
artificial respiration to the words I write.
All day I get impatient
with the light. I need the dark to think certain
thoughts: you buried alive, trapped, blind
in a cave so deep only I know to find you;
resourceful as water,
I bathe and baptize you in similes, teach your eyes
once again to see. Thanks to my caesuras' CPR
you survive. Every night my hand returns
to your chest, my kiss saves your lungs
too parched to care they fill with *my* breath,
every adjective a secret
whispered in your hair, every adverb vicariously
making love to you every prepositional phrase
a rendezvous.

From: virginpoet<virginpoet@>gmail.com>
To: lincolnbraxton<braxtonl@gmail.com>
Subject: Sonnet assignment
Date: Wed, Oct 1, 2003 10:13 p.m.
Attachment And darkly bright bright in dark

Dear Freud:

I expected more from you. You can't accuse a kid of stalking another kid if they're assigned Calculus together and World Religions and German 4 and P.E. . It's not my fault I was given a locker near you. Multiply the number of school days by the years we shared study hall, and you get an idea of how much time I've devoted to gazing at your face. Almost as much as memorizing the endless permutations of sun in the leaves? It vanishes without leaving any trace. Who expects it to be grateful? To be kind? To be true? Okay, I confess. When I talk about light, I mean you.

Not Just A Dangling Participle

Regard said kiss to which I alluded
not as invasion, but as scientific
investigation, osculation
merely a way to test one kind of reality
against another, an experiment to verify
if what's seen can be substantiated;
if the ocular prove oracular.
I won't be making love to your face as much
as corroborating a hypothesis, your lips
my laboratory. Will they have the bite
of the peppermints you pop like painkillers?
Or a smear of chocolate or a residue
of chalk dust? It's applied science
that draws me to your mouth, not lust.

From: virginpoet <virginpoet@>gmail.com>
To: lincolnbraxton <braxtonl@gmail.com>
Subject: Sonnet assignment
Date: Thurs, Oct 2, 2003 7:45 pm
Attachment: For I am shamed by that which I bring forth

Dear Linc,
If we send e-mails back and forth, that's okay? But if we swap sonnets, we might as well be exchanging body fluids? It's a short hop, skip, and jump from similes to sex?
A lost cause, a virgin

Go fuck yourself? No matter how flexible
I am, I can't manage to twist myself
into the right knot. Anyway it isn't me
I want. ***I*** always has a ***you*** in mind. It isn't my
body I take in my arms whenever I take myself
in my arms, but more a twin, who, separated at
birth
from his brother, now wishes again to share
the same skin and crawl back in
to their mutual zygote. I'm not that far removed
from the only Paradise I've known, only a
pronoun
between me and it. *Let me confess we two must
be twain...*
In our two loves there is but one respect.
Why not
return to Eden, in your/my familiar arms
so intimate we'll not tell cause from effect?

From: virginpoet <virginpoet@gmail.com>
To: lincolnbraxton <braxtonl@gmail.com>
Subject: Sonnet assignment
Date: Sat, Oct 4, 2003 6:15 pm
Attachment: Let me not to the marriage of true minds

Maybe, because I suspect you'll not respond to my advances, I make them, but only from miles away. Because you don't think of me, I'm free to think of you. Because I'm enthralled, I'm at liberty to undress you, night after night, yet never lift a hand. To actually caress you would be to turn you into a *you* I'd not recognize.

Love is not love/Which alters when it alteration finds.

Do I really expect to get into college by writing
sonnets to a boy three seats ahead of me
and two to the right, as if assigned this desk
not by our teacher but the sun itself?
Does Harvard want to know how light falls
on your wrist at just the right time?
Even NYU lacks interest in your head's tilt
and MIT prefers calculus to rhyme's
shamelessly indiscreet approximations.
If I've decided to devote my life to staring
at the back of your neck I better get used to
disgrace. I don't have light's excuse.
Who's going to blame it for being besotted
with you? Who wouldn't obsess over such a face?

From: virginpoet <virginpoet@gmail.com>
To: lincolnbraxton<braxtonl@gmail.com>
Subject: Sonnet assignment
Date: Sun, Oct 5, 2003 12:01 pm
Attachment: When most I wink, then do mine eyes best see

Dear *star to ever wandering bark,*
I am afraid if you figure out who I am, you'll be disappointed. Anonymous, I am an enigma, an equation to be solved.
Sailor far from port

To go ga-ga over another, one must be in good
shape.
Furtive looks take a toll on the tendons,
the tilting of the head just so, then twisting it back:
lovely, oblivious ***you***, obsessive ***me*** tied in a knot
of sonnets I scribble in my Lit. book where you live
in the margins next to Shakespeare. It's your fault
and his I dropped the ball that cost the game,
preoccupied
as I was, comparing you to daffodil and me to bee.
How do I make sense of his verse except by writing
my own? I'm a sucker for synecdoche, even if
it produces birth defects like the Bard's *speaking*
breast
(see S. 23) or *bosom endeared with all hearts*
I supposed dead (S. 31). Metaphors should come
like medicines, with warnings of their side effects.

From: virginpoet <virginpoet@gmail.com>
To: lincolnbraxton <braxtonl@gmail.com>
Subject: Confession
Date: Mon, Oct 6, 2003 9:02 pm
Attachment: What wretched errors hath my heart committed?

Dear Linc,
What do I want from you? Maybe the real question is why are you still answering my e-mails? As if you needed something besides football, student council, chorus, church, street hockey, even girls. As if you too longed to live separate from your body. In the ether.

In the ether

Sometimes I miss my train home on purpose,
drawn to the terminal like a shade to limbo:
hundreds of fellow ghosts waiting for transport,
a fertile training ground for poets.
Occasionally an old man pulls out his penis
and plays with it like a cat with a dead mouse –
South Station's my Sex Ed. So why was I shocked
by an actual hand massaging my actual
thigh? At sixteen I looked thirteen. Always tired.
It was a point of pride: I fancied myself
a tormented artist and so deprived my body
of creature comforts like food and rest till,
it seemed, any kind word, anyone's lap, would do.
I might as well have held up a sign: *Please molest.*

From: virginpoet <virginpoet@gmail.com>
To: lincolnbraxton<braxtonl@gmail.com>
Subject: More confession
Date: Mon, Oct 6, 2003 10:14 pm
Attachment: And perspective it is best painter's art

Dear Prospero,
Some things you can only admit to yourself if you say them to someone else... an Earl, a teammate, the Cloud. I've never spoken to anyone before about the man who smelled the way I imagined the earth would if one dug deep enough. He seemed to step out of one of those books Shakespeare might have read before he wrote *The Tempest*: a dark, flowering thing taken human shape.
Your Caliban?

Maybe because I didn't smell of the fires
he'd been fighting, the man sat next to me.
Perhaps he didn't want sex as much
as a blessing. With a few kisses
and a little undressing in a dark corner
of the train station maybe I'd prove compliant
as water. He'd walked through flames
to reach here, but now he was on his knees
I couldn't perform the absolution he begged for.
This is not a story I can tell in liberated verse.
Nothing free about it. Betray another
and you must tell your betrayal for years
afterward, bit by bit, doubt by doubt. Shame by
shame, sonnet by sonnet you spit it out.

From: virginpoet <virginpoet@gmail.com>
To: lincolnbraxton <braxtonl@gmail.com>
Subject: Still more confession
Date: Mon, Oct 6, 2003 10:46 pm
Attachment: Devouring time, blunt thou the lion's paws

Dear Linc,
Sorry to swamp you with yet another e-mail. But some things you must say and then stop and start again in a little more detail and then stop and say again. Maybe that's why Shakespeare wrote all those sonnets, why he kept repeating himself. All the man asked was for me to get undressed. So I didn't escape being raped, when I ran; I failed a test. If a kid keeps getting closer to a flame, naturally the fire suspects he'd like to be burned.

Your Redundant Sonneteer

Talk to my guidance counselor? The school nurse?
My football coach? No, I told the stones
at the beach. They knew about getting molested:
sitting there and letting someone fondle them
again and again. The ocean has nothing else to do
but spill against sand. At loose ends, it bears the
land no ill will. Like me, its quarry
just happens to be close at hand.
For once it helped to have read Shakespeare
who knew full well time's fell hand increasing store
with loss and loss with store. I'll have to wait years
to realize how lucky I was. Ask the tides to stop
what they're meant to do? My assailant let go.
For that other predator, the sea, *no* never means
no.

From: virginpoet <virginpoet@gmail.com>
To: lincolnbraxton <braxtonl@gmail.com>
Subject: Sonnet assignment
Date: Thurs, Oct 9, 2003 11:11 pm
Attachment: Till my bad angel fire my good one out

Dear Flame,
Probably I've dumped all this on you because I got scared by how much I longed for your friendship, and so I found myself telling you the very story that'd make it impossible. You want to know what it's like to be me? When I'm writing about fire, I want to hold It in my fist. And so I do.

Your faithful arsonist

Take the match in your hand
like a key. Use it
to open a door. In you. Teach your skin
a lesson it won't forget.
You want to bang your head against a wall?
Try desire. You want to zoom
inside? Try pain. Rub out a flame
in your palm. Let it read your fortune
and burn till it impresses you
with a scar. Be grateful for the hurt.
Bear it till you can bear it
no more. Every time
you close your fist you'll remember
the annealing power of metaphor.

From: virginpoet<virginpoet@gmail.com>
To: lincolnbraxton<braxtonl@gmail.com>
Subject: Sonnet assignment
Date: Fri, Oct 10, 2003 7:27 pm
Attachment: And for this sin there is no remedy

Dear Linc,
Thanks to the Yellow Pages, my father found a psychiatrist who specialized in molested boys the way an auto shop might fix only foreign cars. "Don't expect miracles," the doctor smiled as a mechanic might, running his hand over the hood of an engine that'd most likely need to be scrapped even after he'd done what he could. Such repairs don't come cheap. Dr. H scolds me every time I start to talk about boys. *My lady doth protest too much, methinks* – as if I'm going out of my way to be queer.

Watch out for doctors who quote Shakespeare.

I hate to admit even as the man kissed
my ear, I'd no clue what he was asking me
to do. He told me to go: I went. I should have
read my Shakespeare. Richard III.
Why should a hawk repent? It's not his fault
the mouse makes the mistake
of being succulent. Even a trout
knows not to jump into the bear's jaws.
Even a ferret's aware of the eagle's intent once
ensconced in his claws. Why was I so dumb?
No baby gazelle worries about bad manners,
in the lion's mouth. But in this bathroom stall,
my pants down to my knees – so much
for human evolution! – I, gripped tight
in the talons, kept trying to please.

From: virginpoet <virginpoet@gmail.com>
To: lincolnbraxton <braxtonl@gmail.com>
Subject: Rant
Date: Sun, Oct 12, 2003 8:19 pm
Attachment: You are so strongly in my purpose bred

Dear Linc,
Here's what I've learned from almost a month of doing the same thing every day, you never get it right. Masturbate every night and you'll see. No matter how much you repeat it, it's never the same. That's true for poetry too. But it's even better than beating off because you can do it anywhere.

Guess who?

Want to succeed in high school?
Learn to text during the Spanish-American
War. Pretend to like beer. Smirk
knowingly if the talk turns to sex.
Make an art out of being bored by the square root
of pi, Kierkegaard, and King Lear. Above all,
learn to sulk, sneer, frown, lips vigilant
every hour, every day, all term.
Sanitize yourself after handling too many similes.
Scrub away a sonnet's venereal germs.
If forced to write a poem, use both hands:
one to put down the words,
the other to hide them. Say what you must
and disguise what you can.

From: virginpoet <virginpoet@gmail.com>
To: lincolnbraxton<braxtonl@gmail.com>
Subject: Sonnet assignment
Date: Sun, Oct 12, 2003 8:42 pm
Attachment: Who hast by waning grown

Dear Linc,
Why you? It wasn't fate. One day I just happened to glance up from Julius Caesar and there the light was: turning you far more interesting than any ablative absolute. I've put off signing my name for so long, you'd have thought it was something special, not just

Chaz

Poor soul, the centre of my sinful earth.
Just one line out of 2,156, yet it kept me
from driving off the road, the tragic hero
of my own sonnet cycle. I don't have the stamina
to be stoic, the moral fiber to be queer.
I distrust God, country, school, literature, and,
being neither athlete nor wit, my own gifts.
But a young man must devote himself to a cause;
so for me it's been self-reviling: the one thing
I'm good at. The Bard's a perfect mentor.
If I must be true to something, why not to a toxic
chemistry Shakespeare midwifed:
my innate capacity for rue, rancor, and regret?
Poor soul, the centre of our sinful earth?

From: virginpoet <virginpoet@gmail.com>
To: lincolnbraxton <braxtonl@gmail.com>
Subject: Sonnet assignment
Date: Sun, Oct 12, 2003 9:37 pm
Attachment: But ah thought kills me I am not thought

Dear Linc,
Thank you for not mentioning my e-mails when we were alone in the locker room. Maybe sonnets are not the kind of thing one talks about when naked.

So shall I live supposing thou art true.

German nouns float through sentences
like battleships – *Gewissenchaft, Wirklichkeit* –
when I should be focusing on torpedoes and treaties
for tomorrow's test, but I'm stuck on *Denkenlicht* –
Who decided ***n*** and ***k*** were essential
for thinking? I can't stop thinking how the word
we can't think without is so flirtatious it rhymes
with almost anything: pink, wink, slink,
stink! The thing is, Shakespeare says, I think of you
and think till I think the worst: you'll never think
of me. He must be sitting right behind me in German,
for every time I look at you, I make myself blink.
Ever try not to think what you can't help thinking,
all that rope played out, link by link,
thought with its own predilection to kink?

From: virginpoet <virginpoet@gmail.com>
To: lincolnbraxton <braxtonl@gmail.com>
Subject: Thank you
Date: Mon, Oct 13, 2003 1:12 am
Attachment: Sullen earth sings hymns at heaven's gate

Dear Fellow Rebel Without a Cause,
I can't believe that, knowing what you do, you were still willing to hitch a ride with me. What is it with teenage boys? We talk about everything but what we most need to say. Girls. Trigonometry. Yesterday's game. At least last night we shared a common darkness.

If you're Dean, I'm Mineo

Fog turns even our town Shakespearean
and you and I actors in a film noir, junkies
smoking reefer (actually non-filter Camels),
looking for a street we haven't gone down yet,
a digression
from the plot in which we've been caught, a song
on the car radio to open a door we'll go through
and never turn back. My future's an arm's length
away.
Grabbing it (you!) would be as easy as turning
the dial to a different station, but I suspect
what will most likely prove true: my life
distinguished by a series of failures of nerve.
Though I long for a sickness that promises no cures
instead, I light up a cigarette and hand it to you:
the closest my mouth will ever get to yours.

From: virginpoet <virginpoet@gmail.com>
To: lincolnbraxton <braxtonl@gmail.com>
Subject: Sonnet assignment
Date: Mon, Oct 20, 2003 6:19 pm
Attachment: Enjoyed no sooner but despised straight

Dear Star Traveler,
Thank you for now showing my sonnets to anyone else. What planet did you land from? What private hurt or longing prevented you from turning away from my not so private hurts and longings.
Sublunar

Who makes a career out of the closet? Or worse,
sonneteering. Neither occupation has a pension
plan, prospects in sight, or room for advancement.
I am that I am. In the middle of the sonnets
Shakespeare flexes his biceps like Popeye:
If you don't like me or my pentameter, scram!
But what if you're an ordinary guy whose only true
muscles are those needed to sigh and study
the backs of boys' necks, memorizing
every hair on their heads? Why can't the eyes be
more practical? What vocation do they aspire to:
gawkers, amateur poets, wannabe queers?
Bring quatrains to a college interview? Not even
Ivy League schools recruit closeted sonneteers.

From: virginpoet <virginpoet@gmail.com>
To: lincolnbraxton<braxtonl@gmail.com>
Subject: Sonnet assignment
Date: Thurs, Oct 23, 2003 10:30 pm
Attachment: Past reason hated as a swallowed bait

Dear Lincoln,
I know, being *gay* doesn't mean being tormented by impossible longings. But being *me* does!

I tried!

Last night I decided to be one of those shadows
that claims a streetlight and waits for a man
lonely enough to roll down his car window.
but when a station wagon door opened,
I fled. There was a rag doll and a rattle on the floor,
not the gnarled ropes I'd hoped for,
nor the Shakespearean dark I'd counted on
turning me so dazzling my captor wouldn't notice
I smelled like cheese allowed to go bad.
I didn't wish to be raped by anyone who drove
the same car as my dad; dirt under his nails.
I wanted to be undressed by hands that moved
as shadows did, taking my measure so lightly
only afterward would I know I'd been caressed.

From: virginpoet <virginpoet@gmail.com>
To: lincolnbraxton <braxtonl@gmail.com>
Subject: Sonnet assignment
Date: Thurs, Oct 23, 2003 11:40 pm
Attachment: To shun the heaven that leads to this hell

Dear Achilles,
After chickening out, I couldn't retreat back home and tell my father "Sorry I wasn't really at a friend's but waiting for a car to stop and a door to open so I could step in and never be the same." I certainly couldn't tell my shrink, who was just waiting for any excuse to laugh at me. So I rode underground till it was time for school. I keep changing subway lines, pretending I was coming from somewhere very important and heading somewhere just as important.

Odysseus

Is this what it's like to die? Doors open
and you sit down next to strangers
on a car carrying you so far underground
there's nothing to see but darkness
rushing past you, though it's really you rushing
past it till you forget where you are.
So this is death? Staring out a window
at a wall and seeing *you* staring at *you*
staring at you for miles and miles.
You wander from one day into the next
without leaving your seat. You plunge under
a river and, if dead, don't even have to
hold your breath. Thanks to all that track,
you don't have to look forward or look back.

From: virginpoet <virginpoet@gmail.com>
To: lincolnbraxton <braxtonl@gmail.com>
Subject: Sonnet assignment
Date: Fri, Oct 24, 2003 8:40 pm
Attachment: And that is this and this with thee remains

Dear Linc,
Hardly an heroic act: typing poems and e-mailing them into the ether. What was I thinking would come from all these attachments. There are so many obligations to being beautiful, and I'm grateful you handled yours with grace and compassion. I got lucky. Maybe someday I'll get up the nerve and fall in love with a boy –or girl – whom I can actually hold in my arms.

Forever in your debt

I admire those aging thespians, the demonstratives
as they slip off and on the stage,
minor characters, who even when they die,
only give a small gasp, this arranged marriage
of ***t*** and ***h***, teeth and tongue so smitten
with each other they turn the breaths I take
in the mirror into this or that, cloud, then clarify
to nothing the way invisible ink vanishes
in the page as soon as it's written.
I'm thoroughly tired of my ambitions
and language's. *This* is not *that*
surprising: one deep sigh and I'll disappear.
Without a trace. As obligingly as an adverb
in the glass, a little superfluity erased.

From: virginpoet <virginpoet@gmail.com>
To: lincolnbraxton <braxtonl@gmail.com>
Subject: Dorm application: Fall 2004
Date: Mon, Oct 27, 2003 11:02 pm
Attachment: Fair, kind, and true, is all my argument

Dear Linc,
What will my children do when they grow up and discover their father's even odder than they suspected. If I'm lucky enough to have kids, I'll know my duty: face to face with beauty, I'll scrub behind its ears. Some may complain of being repressed, I'll be glad my mind's still free to pursue the *ideal* while my hands scrupulously towel off the *real* that always leaves a ring around the tub.

On my dorm application, in the blank for religion,
what if I type *Idolatry*? Will the university
revoke my scholarship if I worship underwear
ads, the shining, long arms and legs that swim
across *Sports Illustrated* covers? Asked
for my roommate preference I quote Shakespeare:
Fair, kind, and true have often lived alone
Which three, till now, never kept seat in one?
Will the Dean assume I want a roomie
with DID? Will I be persecuted for my faith?
I'm at the age I need words to see what we can
together get away with, neither of us too old
to be reckless. The words beg me to type them; I do
like the Bard live dangerously, at least on the page.

From: virginpoet <virginpoet@gmail.com>
To: lincolnbraxton <braxtonl@gmail.com>
Subject: Honors math
Date: Wed, Oct 29, 2003 11:02 pm
Attachment: When beauty lived and died as flow'rs do now

Dear X,
If only I'd developed a crush on a nasturtium. Flowers don't care if anyone ogles them. All day the tulips stare into space like models paid to hold their poses. For hours they memorize the air. No one goes into therapy for stalking gladiola or writing poems to daffodils. Maybe someday I'll show these sonnets to the one with whom I hope to spend the rest of my life. If he or she is still willing to put up with me, then I'll know I have the right person.
Your faithful Y

If I = me someday at 43 > < me now at 18 (locker
#28), then thee = 18 year old you (locker #29)
(if still alive at 43 too) < > *you* and *you*
and *you* (i.e. every boy that reminds me of you,
variable I plug into a formula I'm still trying
to figure out) > < *thee* (Shakespeare's 300 year-old
young man = real Earl + hyperbole), **then** I've an
advantage
over the Bard: I've time to work on these equations:
Yet what of thee thy poet doth invent
He robs thee of, and pays it thee again.
Thank *you*, interchangeable integer, for being *thou,*
my differential lover, most accommodating
of conundrums, providing both the Bard and me
lovely axioms to obsessively sigh and puzzle over.

From: virginpoet <virginpoet@gmail.com>
To: lincolnbraxton <braxtonl@gmail.com>
Subject: Manifesto
Date: Sun, Nov 2, 2003 7:12 pm
Attachment How to divide the conquest of thy sight?

Dear Worried,
I haven't written because I've been too busy trying to end a war. No, that's not quite true. I chose to go to D.C. to prove to myself that I could act on at least one of my convictions. Little did I know I'd end up with a bunch of kids who decided the way to protest the war was to take off their clothes.

Shy Ecdysiast

If the trees on the Esplanade, this Fall, cast off
their underwear, why shouldn't we?
No bolder manifesto than penises flapping
in a breeze, breasts making it difficult
for the cops to decide where to grab.
We're roots and branches but no leaves.
We refuse to be bullied by anything
as bourgeois as shirts and pants.
What fun! It's not only a protest
but a strip tease. We've no allegiance to anything
but light. Even inhibited, timid *I*
throws bare buttocks in the path
of the tanks and that other armed vehicle, the sun.

From: virginpoet <virginpoet@gmail.com>
To: lincolnbraxton<braxtonl@gmail.com>
Subject: Sonnet assignment
Date: Tues, Nov 4, 2003 11:20 pm
Attachment: And captive good attending captain ill

O Captain, my Captain,
The Bard buried a son. Maybe that's why he devoted so many sonnets to the Earl's beauty. *Time's valiant, conscripted dead.* Bring the Bard to the ramparts. I might as well have worn a dress. If this was the 1960s I have been drummed out of the SDS. My parents fought for civil rights. I'm trying to free iambs from centuries of being oppressed. What better way to understand pentameter than by sabotaging it?

From the ramparts!

If fleeing cops, I recommend verse
muscularly gay; its sweetly vain
and surprisingly resilient beloved having survived
Cromwell, Napoleon, Hitler, Ho Chi Minh, LBJ,
and hopefully George Bush and Saddam Hussein.
Gassed, I haven't the stomach for Foucault or
Derrida. The world already deconstructs
if you're breathing chloropicrin bromobenzyl
cyanide: every manifesto now
turned irrelevant as a clock and every key
despairing of its lock. Time pulls on its gas mask
and picks up its club, but at least
in my hands and Shakespeare's, words negotiate,
they work out their differences in rhyme.

From: virginpoet<virginpoet@gmail.com>
To: lincolnbraxton<braxtonl@gmail.com>
Subject: Spanish Lesson
Date: Sun, Nov 23, 2003 6:14 pm
Attachment: Love is not love/Which alters

Que esfuerz del caballo por serperro!
I don't know much Spanish but that doesn't stop me from sitting on the floor and reading Lorca to a fifth grader who by now must be used to suburban kids showing up nightly to tutor him, even though Felix doesn't really care who the 26th President was or who won last year's Super Bowl. So what are we supposed to do for the hour he's agreed to endure so I feel I'm making a difference in the world?
Que grande, que invisible, que diminuto

So what if the horse is trying to squeeze into a dog
and the dog's trying to grow wings and the swallow's
jealous of bee. Lorca's a riddle, Felix and I decide.
We've been reading *Muerte*
in a vault in a bank turned tutoring center.
Felix has told his mother he's studying history
but really he's here to make fun of my crazy accent
and send ships sailing through
sketchbooks, each deck a factory, crowded with men
smelting, weaving, hammering, hoisting. *It's okay.*
Keep reading, he says. *My hands don't care*
what my ears are doing.
And so his freighters rock in the swells of Lorca's
verse and I go home afterward and dream of Federico
lying, feverish in my arms,
and no matter how hard I try
I can't wake him from his nightmare; no matter how
softly I stroke his damp hair, I can't make him suffer
any less. And Felix?
What does he dream of who'd sent such industry,
full sail, towards the horizon?

From: virginpoet<virginpoet@gmail.com>
To: lincolnbraxton<braxtonl@gmail.com>
Subject: Sonnet assignment
Date: Mon, Nov 24, 2003 9:17 pm
Attachment: Love is not love/Which alters

Dear Faithful Reader,
What kid my age and in his right mind locks himself up in a cage, claustrophobic with flowers, birds, and stars? Yet, night after night, I find myself crawling between its bars. For extra credit. Yet here's one of the fringe benefits of infatuation. I'm forced to think up metaphors for your eyes. They hold the galaxies in place. Maybe the Bard's no more queer than I. He's just teaching his beloved a geometry lesson: how much room you can make in a tight space.

Your Faithful Author

Shoot hoops with a son of my own? Perhaps
as unlikely as being drafted by the pros.
No matter how often I dribble in the driveway
I've no illusions I'll make it to the NBA,
though that doesn't stop me from scraping ice
off the blacktop and shooting 100 free
throws in the snow. The hardest part of a lay-up
is letting go what the body wants so to follow
through the air. Some things you wish even
though you guard against letting yourself wish
for them. Imagine playing one-on-one
in the dark with a son till neither of us could see
the ball fall through the net. To keep score
we'd have to listen for the swish.

From: virginpoet <virginpoet@gmail.com>
To: lincolnbraxton <braxtonl@gmail.com>
Subject: Farewell
Date: Wed, Nov 26, 2003 7:12 pm
Attachment: O truant Muse, what shall be thy amends?

Dear Lin,
I worry about you too. Senior Class President, Football Captain, Homecoming King, Merit Scholar, Early Admissions to Princeton, First Prize, State Choir. And beautiful to boot. And kind. And true. A boy with a conscience. A boy with a spine. What does life have left for you? Thanks for letting me come out of the closet while crawling right back at the same time.

Both cursed and blessed.

Enough is enough, says the light, each evening,
fed up with its chores. By day's end,
it's got little left to spend. It's wasted
almost its entire fortune and on what?
A girl's fingernails, a boy's wrist, a bead of dew?
It's got better things to do
than make things shine: a pencil's metal ring,
lip of glass, a kid's cowlick.
Do we expect it to scrimp on the roses
or you? Even the light gets tired
of being a pimp. Enough is more
than enough. The sun's got other concerns.
It can't devote all its energies on you: it's
burning up, old suicide. We must make do.
It's through. For the night. I'm done too.

From: virginpoet <virginpoet@gmail.com>
To: lincolnbraxton <braxtonl@gmail.com>
Subject: Farewell
Date: Wed, Nov 26, 2003 7:12 pm
Attachment: Be thou Tenth Muse, ten times more in worth

Dear Fair, Kind, and True,
Maybe I've been more faithful to the sonnets' tradition than I'd guessed. Thanks to them and you for giving yet another young man – me! – an excuse to indulge in hyperbole.

Enthralled, Enchanted, and Enslaved

How long did I plan to write sonnets
to you? Almost a half century spun from
my computer and flung into the ether
to trap you. A web a far more crafty weapon
than gun or knife. It clings. Similes do that. Stick
to any surface. I feel the tug of a few strands
and I sting. Sonneteers are a perverse crew,
shrewd as any spider. They'll latch
onto you any way they can.
All they need is distance. And words – their
remarkable adhesion. That's how
we poets prey on the unsuspecting:
we stake out your neighborhood.
We make you stay by staying far enough away.

From: virginpoet <virginpoet@gmail.com>
To: lincolnbraxton <braxtonl@gmail.com>
Subject: Happy Thanksgiving
Date: Thurs, Nov 27, 2003 9:20 pm
Attachment: Past reason hunted, and no sooner had

Dear Pilgrim,
Did it never cross your mind – maybe just once? – to call my bluff? What if you agreed to meet in a place where we could try anything? Or maybe we've already found that place. Who needs a parked car on a deserted road when you can steam up the windows of a sonnet?

Squanto

Do not let me reach my arms around you
where your wings ought to be.
Do not let me loosen your shirt, button
by button giving up their allegiances. Stop me
from making love to your collarbone, its
elegant articulations with sternum and scapula.
Forbid my tongue from teaching your nipples
a new usefulness. Keep me
from pulling you slowly down as if you were
an ambushed wave I'd embraced
and refused to let go till I felt the weight
of the whole sea upon me. Do not let me
be adjective to your noun, adverb
to your verb. Do not (oh do!) let me drown.

From: virginpoet <virginpoet@gmail.com>
To: lincolnbraxton <braxtonl@gmail.com>
Subject: Grammar Lesson
Date: Sat, Dec 13, 2003 4:40 pm
Attachment: So long as men can breathe or eyes can see

Dear Proper Noun,
I took the first ten sonnets I sent you – yes, I admit I saved them – and discovered that they averaged 18.6666... nouns; 17.6666... verbs (yes, those 666s proof I'm going to hell, with the help of past and present participles). Yet only 7.2 adjectives,; and 3.0 adverbs. Apparently you don't need all that much modification. So I offer you this early Christmas present, a stocking full of prepositions. Maybe parts of speech do hold the secret to our lives.

Your Faithful Pronoun

Up
Down
In
Out
Over
Under
Before
After
With
Without
Because of
In spite of
In light of
For the love of

From: virginpoet <virginpoet@gmail.com>
To: lincolnbraxton <braxtonl@gmail.com>
Subject: Merry Christmas
Date: Thurs, Dec 25, 2003 7:12 pm
Attachment: Sweets grown common lose their dear delight

Merry Christmas
Years from now when nothing seems to be going right in your life, think of me imagining you. No matter what tests you faced, how disappointed you were in yourself, the light always managed to find you. And so did I. We know the troubled history light brings – of grief and longing – and yet we pledge ourselves to it, both day and night.
And To All a Good Night

After all the double entendres Shakespeare's
been drubbing into us we need a thorough
scrubbing, so
Cupid immerses his heart-inflaming brand
in a bucket and the Bard takes what he's made
beautiful and says, *fuck it* to every rule, all his
mixed
metaphors and warnings against VD swamping us
with a song so garbled it wipes away all memory
of the music that came before, proving
he's not just crude but cruel. Even as the Bard's
enforcing the law, he's breaking it. We're left
scolded. Scalded. Soused. ***FINIS?*** Erase
the word, write it again. Even as we hope for its
Latin
to burst into flame, we're regretting its cooling,
its embers. No noun without its denouement.

From: virginpoet <virginpoet@gmail.com>
To: lincolnbraxton <braxtonl@gmail.com>
Subject: Not done quite yet
Date: Wed, Dec 31, 11:59 p.m.
Attachment: So is the time that keeps you as my chest

Dear Linc,
Look in your glass and there appears a face/ That overgoes my blunt invention quite/Dulling my lines and doing me disgrace. If someone were to come upon my – our! – sonnets, here's what I imagine he or she would think. One, that I was seventeen. Two that I'd little sense there was any verb but the present tense.

You thought I was done, didn't you?

2003 in Review: A ship drops out of the sky.
Colin Powell proves he can lie. Approximately
125,000 children in Darfur learn to die.
In Italy 350,000 year old footprints found.
In Yevpatoriya Cosmic Call sent to Ursa Major.
In Tikrit, Saddam Hussein's fair prey.
In Boston a high school senior, worries he's gay,
goes underground. Kinzua Bridge falls down.
Aug 1, suicide bomb kills 50 in Chechnya hospital.
Nov. 12, suicide bomb kills 22 in Nasiriya.
And, every evening, my sonnet makes light
find its way over galactic miles and years
back to your face, and for that moment
there is no other time, no better place.

From: virginpoet<virginpoet@gmail.com>
To: lincolnbraxton<braxtonl@gmail.com>
Subject: Sonnet assignment
Date: Thurs, Jan 1, 2004 1:11 am
Attachment: O blame me not if I no more can write

Sir Lincoln Braxton,
So our little feast of sonnets you never asked for comes to an end, each course seasoned with puns, more metaphors than you'd ever want to stuff your face with, and a little irony to cleanse your palate. Don't worry about the after-taste.
Sir Charles Winthrop

Because life will surprise us more
than any metaphor. Because we'll discover war's deadly
tedium or the tedium of a glorious cause.
Because we'll let our fathers and ourselves down.
And our fathers will betray us by dying.
And we'll fail our children no matter how hard we try.
Because friends will suffer in ways we'd never guess
and we will not be able to stop this suffering.
Because what we hoped for will not happen
and what will happen we did not hope for.
Because eventually everything's out of our hands.
Because we'll find love, lose, and find it again,
and because we will never truly understand
what words labor so hard to make us understand.

From: virginpoet <virginpoet@gmail.com>
To: lincolnbraxton <braxtonl@gmail.com>
Subject: Sonnet assignment
Date: Fri, Jan 2, 2004 9:36 pm
Attachment: Who will believe my verse in time to come

Dear Linc,
Than you shall hear the surly sullen bell/ Give warning to the world that I am fled. Why should the world want to know about a boy who, for a marking period one fall, chose to believe he was a poet just because he'd fallen in love with light – no, wanted to be laid by it? In the midst of wars and earthquake when this wannabe Shakespeare should've been saving if not the world, at least his chemistry grade, he was mangling iambs rather than isotopes. What normal eighteen-year-old boy longs to make love to light? I did. I thought we all could be saved by tropes.
Chaz

Now that *wild music burthens every bough*
and it's okay to be gay and every adjective's free
to have a fling, I find it less enticing
to turn a thing as intimate as breath into a thing
public as song. When it's so easy to sing
it's time to shut up. Now no one's restricted
I need fetters. I've no hope of being unconflicted
as light. I'm used to the closet's nuances,
a dark I can count on, all those shadows
the sun puts down as a deposit, a blank page's
privacy, rhyme's slammed door, every stanza
a room I've the keys for, my only confidante:
metaphor. Everyone's throwing open the shutters
hiding nothing, and I want to hide even more.

3

My dear fellow, let me advise you not to waste your time over the Sonnets. I am quite serious. After all, what do they tell us about Shakespeare? Simply that he was the slave of beauty.

Oscar Wilde

Perhaps total immersion in the Sonnets -- that is to say, in Shakespeare's mind --is a mildly deranging experience to anyone...

Helen Vendler

The Parting of Raphael and Tobias – Biliverrt – 1680

When my father discovered my desk full of children
with wings, he did what any worried parent might
in a small New England town:
he checked the yellow pages: celestial beings –
especially naked ones – posed
particular problems for a Unitarian-Universalist
like my dad, so it proved
no small task to track down a psychiatrist
who specialized in boys like me.
It'd taken months to collect that many winged
messengers though I left the upper echelons
of archangels to their important
commissions and stole only angels
who wouldn't be missed, the lower ranks
of cherubim, a civil service of seraphim, feathery
lads who couldn't afford full robes
but wore loose fitting sashes always about to
slip from their waists, a heavenly host
obviously still in puberty like me
though apparently not with the same worries
about halitosis and nocturnal emissions.
Commonwealth Avenue doctors handed me back
and forth as if I wasn't just possessed
but pigheaded. Perhaps
the Spanish Inquisition had good intentions
too, but I wasn't about to betray my collaborators:
the curly-haired angel with whom Tobias fell in love,
the bare-shouldered one
who cradled Saint Anthony's head in his lap;
the one swooping down
to stop the blade from Isaac's throat;

the skinny kid battling reptiles
and rodents with human heads
as if aerial warfare with the seven deadly sins
was part of any normal boy's life.
Ever since I can remember
I've been searching strangers' faces,
checking backs for wings, young men
and women with bodies not fully committed
to being mortal. Who couldn't benefit
from an annunciation here,
a warning there, a little divine intervention?

Las Meninas – Velasquez – 1656

You open one of your mother's old art books
and suddenly you're in the King's Palace
wearing the Pooh Bear pajamas
your ex-girlfriend gave you for a joke
and posing for your portrait
while Velasquez shrinks highness and consort
to figures in a mirror on a back wall.
Having painted both Bacchus and Pope Innocent,
he's ready for anything, brush in hand,
leaning sideways, as if it's no big deal
to have someone with Kanga and Roo slippers
teleported into his studio.
Velasquez already has little Princess Margarita
and her cousins to contend with
and her dog, though it, at least, sits demurely.
The Infanta's maids-in-waiting fuss –
Here, drink this, princess, it will soothe your throat –
and she produces that look on her face
little girls sometimes get
with the whole world meant for their amusement.
What must it be like to be five and accompanied
everywhere by an entourage of clowns
and midgets? Young Nicolisto
pokes the sleepy mastiff
and old Mari-Barbola in her dark velvet
grimaces as if she knows what the Infanta will learn
all too soon. With a few strokes
the painter does what would require the blood
of a hundred revolutionaries; everyone's equal
in the painter's eyes: mastiff, spinster dwarf, Philip IV,
even a kid in his Winnie the Pooh pajamas.

What a triumph: to paint yourself painting
the King of Spain, as long as you hold a brush
in one hand and a palette in the other,
free, not just with his royal majesty but
with light itself. To take the same vicarious pleasures
it does. Gold vermillion, rose madder,
Naples yellow, zinc white, and alizarin crimson.

The Triumph of Bacchus – Velasquez – 1628

It's not that hard to steal a Roman god
from a museum library: you just cough
loud enough to cover the sound of paper objecting
to its tearing and then fold Bacchus
into threes and slip him
under your belt, some paintings meant for more
than seeing, and this boy's a grape so plump
I almost pop him into my mouth
before I stuff him down my trousers.
I didn't come expecting to abscond
with this slightly flabby god,
but I'm not going to leave him to wallow
inside the book. My fingers want to be free
to tweak his left nipple
or squeeze where his biceps should be
if he'd spent more time working out
and less hanging with men
who, old enough to be his father,
cradle their bowls of wine and smirk
as if they're about to try something
they've decided they can get away with.
Outside the museum, art lovers
of another sort have taken refuge from the cold
in as many coats as possible,
drawn from all parts of the city to the sun
on the wide steps leading up to Venus
and Apollo. When I hurry past
the men look up from their paper-bagged bottles
just as the roisterers in the Velasquez do,
staring straight out of the picture.
I have Bacchus in my pants. For now
I've got everything I need.

Tutorial in the Metaphysical Poets

1 *News from a foreign country came*

Why don't you take off your shirt?
I'm learning the art of massage and yours
is the perfect body to practice on –
such a cheesy line to come from a man
with a chair endowed in his name.
Did my professor intend to give up Richard Crashaw
for back rubs, Sir John Suckling
for latissimus dorsi, Andrew Marvell
for rhomboideus major and minor?
Say no to the author of books so expensive
only libraries could buy them?
I was already intoxicated with after-dinner liquors
and *They are all gone into the world of light.*
If my teacher needed my back
to experiment on, didn't I owe him that much?
Here, let me help you. He undid my buttons
as if I were a child who hadn't learned
to get undressed on his own
or a son being readied for his bath.
My professor's office was small but its dark
huge. I expected the walls to open
the way they do in planetariums
to a universe waiting to be admired.
This man who knew maybe more than anyone
about the seventeenth century
didn't have time to waste
on whole sentences. *Please,*
he begged my shoulders. *Please,*
he confided to my ribs.

2 *So let us melt and make no noise*

Not till he unlaced and slipped off my shoes
and rolled down my socks
did I realize lovemaking might commence
with the heel. Was he searching
to see if if I might actually be a goddess's son
dipped in an immortal stream?
My right, then my left foot arched
the way a stroked cat might.
My professor began deconstructing me.
toe by toe. It might've been creepy
if it hadn't felt so good.
Nothing in my high school Sex. Ed class
had prepared me to erupt in orgasm
from having my ankles caressed.
Afterward, he studied my semen
as if every thread of it merited close observation
the way one holds a spider's web to the sun
to test how far it might stretch.
Maybe I'd not prove a complete disappointment
to him. Hands that had authored
Donne and The Great Chain of Being
now committed themselves to my solar plexus;
a textual analysis of my rib cage;
a lengthy exegesis on my inner elbow;
my eyelids and nose delineated;
my collar bone explicated;
my underarms
a small digression, apparently nothing of me
found wanting. I was young.
Who knew what surprises
my body might have left?

3 *...my striving eye/Dazzles at it, as eternity*

When I woke up, I had a blanket tucked around me
like a shipwreck survivor, not a freshman
who couldn't locate his underwear
and so put on his teacher's. I must've looked like a kid
wearing his daddy's boxers,
holding them up by the waist as I felt my way
from one dark room to another,
Professor, I kept whispering, *Professor,*
where are you? It seemed unthinkable
to address a man thrice my age
by his first name even though he'd just invested
his DNA in me. *Professor?*
He slept so determinedly on the couch
I didn't have the heart to wake him.
When I think of that night –
and I think of it often – I remember the moon
lending his belly and thick arms
a sheen that water might have envied.
The afghan he'd kicked loose
I drew back over him, running my hand
through his hair. *Like gold to airy thinness beat.*
Now that he had tired of doing what he wanted
with my body, it was my turn
to do what I liked
with his. Was this why I'd let someone older
than my father mount me?
So when he fell asleep
I'd be free to play with his chest hair,
straightening each strand and letting it spring back,
finally intimate with a man
in ways I'd never dared,

his arms flung out, hands
fluttering as if in his dreams he was swimming.
I could even appreciate the penis more
now that it wasn't trying so hard.
How like an angel came I down.
At last I could gaze at a man as I might
at a tree or pond,
look without looking away.

4 *Hark, hard, the waters fall, fall, fall*

Not his mouth nibbling my neck and shoulders
as if determined to swallow my entire body

starting with the smoothest parts of me;
not his arms holding down mine

as if I were a kid throwing a tantrum.
No, what I remembered

is how patiently his fingers proceeded
down my shirt,

as if showing me how to perform
the simplest of acts: undo

what once required practice to learn:
forefinger easing down, thumb waiting below

like movers managing something unwieldy
they didn't want to drop.

I stayed as still as I could. I tried
to take in everything he was teaching.

5 *When Thou hast done, Thou hast not done*

At the door, I fiddled with my sneakers
like a three-year-old learning to tie a knot.
Only a half an hour before
a world authority on Dryden had found me
so important he left something
of himself inside me. In one night my Ptolemaic world
turned Copernican. I'd not known
minutes could stretch the way sonnets could.
But flat on a desk
with George Herbert nudging my spine
and the Dean of St Paul's for a headrest
I had understood the music of the spheres
for the first time and believed
the moment could last a lifetime
though it proved done
almost as soon as it had begun.

6 *...like a great wing of pure and endless light.*

When the man ran his hands over my back
as if measuring for wings
I knew more would be asked of my body

than it had thought itself capable,
my arms stretched
till I almost expected them to sprout feathers,

my legs ready to abandon the earth.
Pressed down I'd been exalted;
gripped tight, I knew

any moment those arms might tire of me
and I'd plummet to the Earth:
Icarus spilling out of Daedulus' embrace.

Afterward, helped to my feet
and steadied as if I'd forgotten how to walk,
I was dismissed. I didn't mind.

A seed had been planted so deep in me
I knew it would take root.
What English major gets a chance like that:

to know what angels must know
every day of their existence:
the great ring of pure and endless light?

I had the rest of my life ahead of me
to remember.
That ought to be enough for any mortal.

Rorschach Test in the Psych Ward

It's a bramble, I told the doctor.
Only wrens and sparrows find their way into it.
They sing to their heart's content there.
Because I had to pass through a locked door
to look at picture cards the doctor displayed
for me, I was careful not to say
what I really saw in case he might not let me out,
my eyes always trying to make life difficult
for me. A spider bloated from swallowing its children
became a flowering bush; a man holding his penis
a wounded ferret. I turned the boy with breasts
into a very old woman combing her hair;
a father with a knife in his hand
into a penitent carrying a Bible.
The most famous prostitute of all history
hung on the wall
next to my psychiatrist's Harvard diploma –
my pain nothing
compared to Mary Magdalene's.
Did the hospital believe its mentally ill patients
might benefit from a little art history?
Was Mary part of the test
my parents had sent me here to take?
In her lap a skull;
on her dressing table opened pages
and a lamp reading them intently;
in her hands a brush;
her blouse white, her skirt scarlet;
the candle reflected in her mirror
equally schizophrenic – the painter
about as subtle as Freud.
No one, after lighting a lamp
covers it with a vessel or stores it under a bed,

but sets it on a stand
that those who enter may see the light.
For nothing hid that shall not be made manifest,
Later I discovered Georges De la Tour
painted several Magdalenes and the smoking flame,
each slightly different –
the book placed this way or that;
the blouse falling off the shoulder
or accentuating the cleavage;
her hands folded
or her chin resting on her palm;
candle providing the luminescence in one picture,
an oil lamp in others – but all
committed to the same wistfulness,
the same concentration of shadows,
so many rich variations to a common darkness.

A Shower on the Bridge between Trenton and
Morrisville

The cops left the rain in charge
of crowd control and now we are so drenched
what's the point of packing up?
It's too wet to imagine ourselves
anywhere else. The rain won't let our minds
wander. It prolongs its interrogation,
wanting answers, but nothing we say
satisfies it. *Honk for peace,*
we shout like a gaggle of geese
who've made themselves so obvious
drivers have to steer around them.
The worst place to stand in a shower
is on a bridge. Everywhere we turn: weather
with no intention of making this day
any easier for us. Soaked,
there's no comfort to be had
gazing at a river. Look up
and the sky might as well be a lake.
If only the rain were just an old busybody
who, if ignored, might go away
but this munitions factory, assembly-
line worker, assistant district attorney,
muscle-bound methodical downpour?
No one knows better than rain
how to reduce everyone to a common
denominator. What are we doing,
five or six miles north from where Washington crossed
the ice-cold Delaware, forming a human chain
across a bridge whose blinking sign boasts
WHAT TRENTON MAKES THE WORLD
TAKES. The rain exiles all,

takes a beat-up city and beats it
senseless. We hold up placards
that began bleeding at the first drops, no match
for the rain, its familiar, relentless,
uncompromising history lesson.

Missing Classmates

If you have information of their whereabouts...

Where are you, Dexter Winslow,
the only boy to have breasts
in ninth grade, a kid who even in junior high
looked as if he ought to be wearing a pith helmet
and poring over a lost civilization's broken pottery?

Where are you, Ferdinand Coronado,
the new kid with a name so extravagant
we almost expected you to show up,
the first day of school,
wearing a cape and brandishing a saber.

Where are you, Hon Herlihy,
the redneck son of an architect, collar up,
cigarette in mouth, talking
as Elvis would if he'd gone to school
in the shadows of Harvard?

And you Jack Hardy, who in ninth grade spoke French
like a Frenchman and glided from dead heads
to jocks to future senator as effortlessly
as a diplomat, making new teachers feel welcome
as if it was your classroom, not theirs?

And you Robbie Spiller
who used to trip me in the hallways
and then help me pick up my books?
And you, W.B.C.,
who smuggled gold into the country

for a lawyer good enough to get your sister off
for murdering her lover in the elevator
we used to ride up and down your Beacon Hill house.

And you, Lincoln Braxton.
Even Princeton wants to know what happened

to one of the prettiest boys ever to catch a football.
Where are you hiding, Linc?
With all the other ghosts from our class?
Pete Stern, who died before his voice got a chance
to change, or Rob Bancroft,

that gentle Mormon who scored a perfect SAT
and killed himself in the B School parking lot?
And A. J. Rackham ,who tried to steal my girl,
and Phillip Silber, who screwed her
before I got up the nerve to try.

A kid with auburn hair
and the sweetest ass you could imagine
and the name Lincoln Braxton
ought not to be allowed to grow up
only to end in ashes.

I just want to be told you're alive, Linc,
and there's some justice to this world
and you received your fair share of it,
at least some reward for being tough and innocent,
gracious and shy and eager

to be liked, and for speaking to me
that first lunch at our new school
when we knew no one else
and so sat together and told each other things
we'd have told no one else, that day.

Ask the Hummingbird About Self-Promotion

1
Self-publishing?
If the trees don't have any scruples about doing it,
why should I?

2
There's no real reason for the bird to sing
all morning outside my window.
It's just one of its more annoying habits.
The same could be said of me
and yet I return to my computer
as if it expected me as much as the branch does the bird.

3
The dog has no hope of placing his autobiography
on *The New York Times Best-seller List,*
yet he keeps reworking it
as if each tug at his chain deserves a chapter
and surely someone in the neighborhood must be
recording what he's been dictating for weeks.

4
The crickets never seem to feel the need
to revise the one poem
they write over and over, each night.
Apparently they don't mind remaining anonymous.

5
There's that bird again.
Hasn't it heard of a thesaurus?

6
The bluejay pretends he was here for breakfast first.
Such bad manners
how can you not admire him?

7
The chickadees don't discriminate
between major and minor poets.
They eat what anyone scatters.

8
Thanks for thinking of us.
We had so many wonderful submissions
but we couldn't select all.
Tell that to the animals that didn't get picked
for the ark. *Good luck,*
the superfluous monkeys wave to Noah. Meaning:
May you sprout a leak before you sail out of sight.

9
It's raining. It's often raining when I write.
The drops throw themselves against the window.
They want to be in the poem too.
They don't care what it's about.

10
I put aside my pencil and pad.
I pick up a book by Lynn Levin, Elizabeth Raby,
Patricia Goodrich, or Pamela Perkins-Frederick.
Who knows birds better
than poets who've negotiated their own tricky
take-offs, their virtuoso landings.
I read and read Joan Aleshire's *This Far*
or Ellen Bryant Voigt's *Shadow of Heaven*
or Cornelius Eady's *Victims of the Latest Dance Craze*

or Betsy Sholl's *Don"t Explain*
till my feathers are heavy with rain,
my shoulders itch to fly.

11
The trees must have noticed
my attention wandering.
I look out the window to find them
holding up their latest work.
They must've been inspired by Steven Riel,
Luray Gross, or Hayden Saunier.
Their first drafts have turned incandescent.
They're redolent with so many reds –
Persian red, Prussian red, Venetian red,
Congo rubine, Majolica earth –
you need a map as well as a thesaurus
to sail though them; madder yellow,
quince yellow, gamboge, phosphine, saffron –
you could lick the color off the leaves.
While I've been dawdling
the trees have been busy revising.

Is There No Cure?

What are you thinking? you inquire
as we lie in bed. *Oh nothing*, I say, meaning the dark
unraveling of Butler Gartar Snake,
the tough, unbelievably elastic Salt Marsh Snake.
Is it too much to ask you to tolerate the nudes
I've stashed in my desk drawers:
Copper-bellied Water Snake, Gulf-hammock
Rat Snake, Texas Blind Snake?
One can't get much more naked
than Ramphotyphios braminas.
These lithe shimmering bodies might not be grounds
for parting but surely for concern.
If my students knew, would they turn me in to the Dean?
Certainly they'd suspect my focus on comma splices
hid more troubling passions
but there's probably no danger of me showering illicitly
with any under-aged
Mississippi Kite and I'm not likely to get arrested
for yearning to roll in the buff with Abyssinian Genet.
Though it might be awkward
to admit obsessing over Gambon Mongoose
or White-Naped Weasel – their names
as seductive as their fur – at least
I'll not find myself on the Five O'Clock News.
Teacher Confesses to Writing Sonnets
to Sand Cats of Africa!
If only I'd been born with less troubling cravings.
It's hard to get anywhere
if one's always pulling one's car off the road
to gawk at slender, supple bodies
stretching at street corners

making their boredom clear to to the world:
Crape Myrtle. Yellow-tipped Poplar,
Blossoming Apple, showing of their new duds
all elbows and shoulders,
tough talk and trembling
Silk Oak, Alligator Pear, Flowering Almond
still growing into their insatiable thirsts.

John 8:12

It's 2014. One can let children play with fire now
without getting in too much trouble
from their parents. When I give my Sunday School class
battery-operated tealights,
Josie puts hers in her mouth.
She may be in seventh grade but that doesn't stop her
from doing silly things
with light, Maggie slides her candle
under her headband and Tyler's inspired
to slip his inside his shirt pocket.
Look, I've got a breast
that lights up. If only their fathers and mothers knew
what happens when you invite kids
to use their imaginations
with the Bible. Grace closes her fingers
around her candle. Now she's got a fistful of light.
When Jesus said *I am the light,*
was he hoping for this?
Mark turns his tealight off and on
as if he can't quite believe there's such a thing
as a battery-operated candle.
He almost expects the wick to burn him.
He's in fourth grade but he's still puzzled
by many of life's mysteries.
He wants a candle for his baby sister.
He's going to trick Abigail.
He's going to make the light disappear.
She'll want to know where it's gone
and then he'll flick the switch
and there Jesus will be.
He was there all the time.
Josie hands me a picture of a single flame

she's drawn so faithfully
you'd have never guessed
she'd just been chewing light.
You'd swear she'd been studying fire
all her life. The picture is for a friend of mine
who's dying. I am to give my friend
Josie's candle too, teeth marks
and all. Josie isn't worried
if my friend believes in God or not.
She knows she believes in light.

Acknowledgments -II

Thanks for being so true, I could find no words
up to the task of describing you.
Adjectives prostrated themselves at your feet.
Adverbs fainted at the very thought of you.
Nouns, those old pederasts, saw their many advances
rebuffed. And verbs? They gave up long ago
trying to wrestle you down to the page.
Only the pronouns were so foolish
as to think *they* had a chance with *you.*

Thank you for being so kind, I had to summon words
to do you justice and so finally I had a purpose
in life. A boy writes sonnets
to another boy not to persuade him into bed,
but to entangle him in a web.
In high school how often do you get to be an arachnid
and spin and spin so many gauzy
metaphors at last there are enough *likes*
and *as ifs* to lure your subject in?

Thank you for being so fair, you made me grotesque
in comparison. I wasn't writing hyperboles
but emitting them. Hunched over
I could've been mistaken for a spider
pulling similes out of my belly, filaments
that, if tugged too hard, would snap.
I've got to hand it to spiders.
At least they get something for all their effort.
Fair, kind, and true –

that's you. *Ugly, mean, and false*, that's me.
And yet when I was weaving light
through my sonnets, turning certain sounds –
*b'*s or *v'*s or *q*s – into threads
in the tapestry I was weaving out of all the glimpses
I had of you, that quietly embroidered
commotion words make,
I could almost forgive myself my hungers.
These tangled strands I've spun
knotted now I offer you. No hunger, no web.

in memory of

Pamela Perkins-Frederick
Herb Perkins-Frederick
Robert Fraser
Douglas Hughes
Beverly Foss Stoughton
Israel Halpern
Nancy Winter
Jonathan Higbee Bursk

in honor of
Wendy Fulton Steginsky
David Simpson
Wendy Welter Brown
Carolina Morales
Marie Kane
Joan Aleshire
Gerad Schultz
David Kime
D.A. Korcynski

CPSIA information can be obtained at www.ICGtesting.com
Printed in the USA
BVOW07s1220190115

383744BV00003B/4/P

9 781625 491176